Rooted in Jesus

ROOTED IN
JESUS
DEVOTIONS OF VICTORY

LESLIE JACKSON

MINISTRIES

Rooted in Jesus
Copyright © 2022 Leslie Jackson

ISBN: 978-1-7345854-3-8

Cover Illustration by Lacey Ballard
Book Design by Paul Nylander | Illustrada

Printed in the United States of America

For information:
https://LeslieJackson.org
Leslie@LeslieJackson.org

Table of Contents

Table of Contents

Introduction

"God told me to tell you, your roots are growing deeper, and you are beginning to have great fruit," my husband said. Those words on, November 21st, 2021, were a blessing to hear that my passionate pursuit of Jesus was headed in the right direction.

I used to race through life by seeking thrills, eating, drinking, going to work, and looking forward to the weekends. My goal was to be happy. The only thing was, I knew in my soul there was more to life, and I was not on the right track.

How to find the right direction? I decided to *change course*. (See my memoir with this same name.) I took several paths, got into many ditches, had some false starts, and then finally knew I had found the right direction: The living word, Jesus, the rich soil for my soul. I began to grow my roots deep down into my relationship with Jesus.

What is this book? It is the pouring out of my thoughts, feelings, and discoveries as I journey to know my creator on an intimate level. I have been on a "seek and find" mission ever since I was "born again" and my spirit was renewed. God has been gracious and loving in providing answers to my prayers and pleas for understanding as I grow my roots deeper and deeper into Jesus.

A prayer from the Apostle Paul is fitting to start our engines and receive victory through Jesus.

> *"For this reason, I kneel before the Father, from whom his whole family in heaven and on earth derives its name. I pray that out of his glorious riches he may strengthen you with power through his Spirit in your inner being, so that Christ may dwell in your hearts through faith. And I pray that you, being rooted and established in love, may have power, together with all the saints, to grasp how wide and long, and high and deep is the love of Christ, and to know this love that surpasses knowledge — that you may be filled to the measure of all the fullness of God. Now to him who is able to do immeasurably more than all we ask or imagine, according to his power that is at work within us, to him be glory in the church and in Christ Jesus throughout all generations, for ever and ever! Amen."* (Ephesians 3:14–21 NIV)

You will discover the love Jesus has for you while you grow your roots deep within Him, and you will see His miracles and blessings all around you. This book allows readers to focus on defining a new life in Christ Jesus. See yourself in His love and His light as He shines brightly in your life and gives you direction toward your destiny. You will enjoy victory now and for all eternity through Jesus.

Amen. Thank you, Jesus.

Beginnings

"In the beginning was the Word, and the Word was with God, and the Word was God. He was with God in the beginning. Through him all things were made; without him nothing was made that has been made. In him was life, and that life was the light of all mankind. The light shines in the darkness, and the darkness has not overcome it." (John 1:1–5 NIV)

TODAY'S INSPIRATION

For the first part of my life, my biblical knowledge comprised of the first page of the Bible in the book of Genesis and the last page in the book of Revelation, and a few stories in between.

I learned about Adam and Eve's sin in the garden from watching television and from Sunday school. I learned how Moses parted the Red Sea, how Noah built an ark and why we have a rainbow after the rain.

In those early years, I recited the Apostle's Creed and the Lord's Prayer at church every Sunday. I could even recite from memory John 3:16, so I could be confirmed.

I learned all these things, yet they did not mention the name of Jesus at church in a way that caught my attention. I did not truly know Jesus. I had no real depth of understanding of who He was.

In the beginning of my journey in Christianity, like some people, we have meaningful spiritual events that shape our lives. Looking back, my understanding of Jesus in the beginning was not as rich as it is now. It used to be incomplete and dull concerning who the Father, Jesus, and Holy Spirit were in my life. I didn't know them or understand them. Learning about them and growing in my faith didn't happen overnight.

To grow my roots into Jesus, who I desired to know, I had to read the Word of God and meditate on those words. Over time, thankfully, the words began to become real to me and take root within me. If you are new in your faith in Jesus, read the Bible, God's Word, and let God's truths grow into a place of realness in your life.

No matter where you are at on your spiritual journey, especially in the beginning, do not feel condemned.

God meets you where you are and loves you no matter what. There will be times when you miss it, need to dust yourself off, and continue your journey. Keep focusing on Him, His Word and moving forward.

REFLECTION
Does Jesus feel nearer and closer than a best friend? Jesus is always that near. Reflect on His love for you now. Step closer, continue to grow your roots deep into God's word, breathe deeply and feel His love for you, for He is life eternal.

PRAYER

> *Lord, thank you for my life in you. Thank you for your love for me and for saving me. I ask you to help me to always feel your presence and the love you have for me. I ask you to help me see you all around me as I draw closer to you.*
> *In Jesus' name. Amen.*

Why You Need Jesus

"For God so loved the world that He gave His
one and only Son, that whoever believes in
Him shall not perish but have eternal life."
(John 3:16 NIV)

TODAY'S INSPIRATION

For a long time, I thought the purpose of needing Jesus
was just to save me from my miserable self, forgive my
sins, and earn my ticket to Heaven when I died. I think
some of us have misunderstood how to apply the real
meaning of John 3:16. You may have heard this all your
life and are just now wondering what it really means to
have eternal life.

It's true that Jesus died for our sins. It's also true that
if you believe in Jesus, you will not perish, as the Word
says. What if there is much more than just going to

heaven? What if it's about having a personal, relationship with the one who is everything you could ever need in this life and the life to come? There is more. Let me tell you why.

The love of God is the most powerful force on Earth. He gave his love to all of us through Jesus. God is love and everything He does is out of the tremendous love He has for us and His children. He wants you to be His beloved. God calls you to an intimate relationship with Him; a relationship that is deeper and more profound than any other relationship you have, including your mate, a family member, or best friend.

This relationship is available because He sent His son, Jesus. What a tremendous sacrifice and gift he has extended, to be in a relationship with you and me. He says in John 17:3 NIV, *"Now this is eternal life: that they know you, the only true God, and Jesus Christ, whom you have sent"*. It is through faith in Jesus Christ that you find the meaning of eternal life.

The eternal life that He is talking about is one of genuinely "knowing" the one true God and His son Jesus. What a gift you have in Jesus who God sent to us so He would unite you with him in a loving relationship.

Yes, we all want to go to heaven. As believers, we will enjoy an afterlife, our present lives cannot be compared to a life for all eternity in Heaven. The real prize is knowing Jesus so intimately now that you have no fear in this life or the next. Jesus is so wonderful and beautiful that everything and everyone in Heaven is worshipping Him, the King of Kings, and Lord of Lords. Do you want to be a part of this heavenly celebration?

God took away our fear, isolation and eternal darkness that separated us from Himself by sacrificing the thing He loved the most, His son Jesus. A world that wanted nothing to do with Him or knew that they even needed a Savior.

Why do you need Jesus? Because He is the key to your life. He is the life that we all need. Without Him, you will perish and be eternally separate from God. With Jesus, you will no longer be separated from God. You'll never be alone, never be afraid, and never be without His love. You will be firmly rooted in Jesus.

Just like a good earthly father, God wants His children to love Him and know Him. Our heavenly Father God wants you to know Him and His son intimately.

Heaven may be a goal; however the real blessing is knowing Jesus now and for all eternity. The best you can imagine comes from knowing and believing that He is God's son, who came to save the world from eternal damnation and sin. He came so you can walk in freedom and peace with Him. He came so you could be His beloved.

This happens the moment you receive Him into your heart. It happens the moment you say yes to Jesus; then you receive life eternal. Give your life to him today This is clearly stated in the following verse:

> *"And this is the testimony: God has given*
> *us eternal life, and this life is in his Son.*
> *Whoever has the Son has life; whoever does*
> *not have the Son of God does not have life."*
> (1 John 5:11–12 NIV)

REFLECTION

Take a few moments to think about where your heart is with Jesus. Are you far away from Him? If so, He says, *"Here I am! I stand at the door and knock. If anyone hears my voice and opens the door, I will come in and eat with that person, and they with me."* (Revelation 3:20 NIV)

Jesus wants you to accept Him today. He may have been knocking at your door for a long time. Open your heart and receive all He has for you. His love for you will surpass any love you have ever experienced before in this world.

Think about your life with endless love; that is Jesus.

PRAYER

Lord, I receive you now as my Lord and Savior. I believe you are God's Son and that He raised you from the dead. I believe God sent you to die for me and shed your blood for me. I ask you to come into my life and take over. I give you my life. Lead me. Teach me. I ask you to forgive all my sins and wash me clean. I thank you for making me your beloved. In Jesus' name. Amen.

Road to Salvation

"Salvation is found in no one else, for there is no other name under heaven given to mankind by which we must be saved." (Acts 4:12 NIV)

TODAY'S INSPIRATION

If you are on a road with a destination in mind, how do you start? Obviously, you need to know how to get where you are going. You may need a map, GPS (Global Positioning System), or personal guide.

If you want Heaven on Earth and your final destination Heaven, you will also need a guide, which is Jesus. You will need a map, which is the Bible, and you will need wisdom, the precious Holy Spirit, for your journey as you travel here on Earth and to your destination, Heaven.

Merriam-Webster defines salvation as the state of being saved or protected from harm or a dire situation. In religion and theology, salvation refers to the deliverance of the soul from sin and its consequences.

God offered up His Son to us because Jesus was the only way to get back in right relationship with God in this fallen world (see Genesis 3). Jesus is the Way to eternal life. You can't obtain eternal life by being good enough, preaching enough, praying enough, giving enough to your favorite organization, or even going to church enough without Jesus. You must take the correct road and the correct way, which is Jesus.

God's gift of salvation is based on Jesus' sacrificial death. Being rescued is a gift and it is the perfect word when you think about it. If you were drowning and someone came along with a boat, that would be the perfect thing: you need to be rescued. It's the perfect gift.

So it is with salvation, the most incredible life-changing gift you could ever receive. How does this gift save and change you?

After Jesus' sacrificial death, He was miraculously raised from the dead and victorious over Satan and over all sin, sickness, poverty, depression, deep inner heartache, mental pain, fear, and darkness. Jesus paid the supreme and complete price for all offenses humankind would ever make against God. In Jesus, you have the only means for salvation. He is the way, the road map.

When you choose Jesus over Satan and the world, you are victorious and triumphant, just as Jesus was upon his resurrection. This happens when the salvation gift is received, and you are saved for eternity. The scripture below describes what Jesus did to the enemy, Satan.

> *"And having disarmed the powers and*
> *authorities, he made a public spectacle of*
> *them, triumphing over them by the cross."*
> (Colossians 2:15 NIV)

You have been offered the gift of eternal life and a personal relationship with God. You are invited to choose His roadmap for your life. All you need to do is have faith in his Son, Jesus, to start your journey.

Seek Jesus now and secure your salvation – fasten your seatbelt and enjoy the ride.

REFLECTION

What road are you on today? Are you on the road to eternal life? If not, take a week or even a month and think about where your life is going. Ponder on the choices you are making and why you are making them. Reflect on the thought that God loves you and wants to save you. If you are headed in the wrong direction or in the ditch, turn around today, and take the road to Jesus.

PRAYER

> *Lord, I want to choose your way. I turn from my way and turn to your way. Teach me to walk on your road of life. Save me from my sin. Be my perfect gift. Teach me to follow you and not go my own way. I receive all you have for me now and ask you to help me live solely for you. In Jesus' name. Amen.*

Water Baptism

"Therefore, go and make disciples of all
nations, baptizing them in the name of the
Father and of the Son and of the Holy Spirit."
(Matthew 28:19 NIV)

TODAY'S INSPIRATION

Water baptism is one of the most important sacraments
of the Body of Christ. It is a powerful symbol of the old
life being done away with and the new life you live unto
the Lord.

I volunteer at a ministry in downtown Minneapolis
where we meet the natural needs of the people by offering food, clothing and then speak to their eternal needs.
I personally like to sit down with the people, welcome
them and get to know them a little before I share Jesus
with them.

Recently I was at the ministry and I found myself sitting with a man whose first name was Jackson which happens to be my last name. Right away we had a connection with the name Jackson. He had been in the United States for a few years and spoke English well so we were able to communicate. After we laughed about our names and got to know each other, I asked if he knew Jesus. He said he did and was raised a Catholic for many years. He went on to share that everyone in his family was water baptized except him. I asked him if he desired to be water baptized and he said yes.

Then I thought of the story in the bible where the eunuch desired to be baptized. Here is that story.

> *"The eunuch asked Philip, 'Tell me, please, who is the prophet talking about, himself or someone else?' Then Philip began with that very passage of Scripture and told him the good news about Jesus. As they traveled along the road, they came to some water and the eunuch said, 'Look, here is water. What can stand in the way of my being baptized?' And he gave orders to stop the chariot. Then both Philip and the eunuch went down into the water and Philip baptized him. When they came up out of the water, the Spirit of the Lord suddenly took Philip away, and the*

eunuch did not see him again, but went on his
way rejoicing." (Acts 8:34–39 NIV)

Having this bible verse in mind I asked one of
the ministry leaders where they baptized people at in
their ministry and he told me they had not baptized
anyone yet.

In my heart, I knew we had to find a way to baptize
Jackson because if there is a desire for baptism, we need
to honor it in the name of Jesus. We decided to go into
the facilities kitchen and fill a very large bowl with water
and use that. Knowing the location of the baptism was
not the important part, the repentance and desire to
have God the Father, God the Son, and the Holy Spirit
present is what truly mattered.

The baptism was beautiful as the above-mentioned
Bible verses were read and we baptized Jackson. The
water cleansed him from the past, his sins washed away
forever, never to be thought of by God, and became a
new man in Christ. Baptism is an important symbol
of our faith, no matter your age or how long you have
known the Lord.

REFLECTION
Have you been baptized? Jesus loves you and desires
that you be baptized if you have not been already. We

are all His children, and He invites us to come to him. Let your friends know that you are changed after the baptism and living a life for Jesus now. Let's populate Heaven and deplete Hell.

PRAYER

Lord, I thank you so much for cleansing me from all sin and for the power baptism represents in my life. I ask you to help me walk in my new life and this new way. Let my heart always be positioned and focused on you. In Jesus' name. Amen.

The Trinity (Father, Son, and Holy Spirit)

"Then God said, 'Let us make man in our image . . .'" (Genesis 1:26a NIV)

TODAY'S INSPIRATION

God the Father, God the Son, and God the Holy Spirit. Three in one equals The Trinity. In the above verse, God said "us." It's plural, more than one, and what I am calling The Trinity in this devotional.

Below, I will give multiple scriptures to demonstrate how the Bible describes God as three in one.

God and His energy are everywhere. You cannot see the wind, yet you see the movement of the leaves on the trees, so you believe in the wind. God is similar. You cannot see God, yet you can see His goodness as He showers gifts of love upon you when you're willing to see.

> *"Every good and perfect gift is from above,*
> *coming down from the Father of the heav-*
> *enly lights, who does not change like shifting*
> *shadows."* (James 1:17 NIV)

God is all-powerful and loves all His children. Jesus Christ is God's Son, God's "hands and feet" here on Earth. Through His Son Jesus, everything that was made was created through Him. Jesus came to this world in the flesh to be a sacrifice for all eternity so we could reclaim authority over what we lost because of sin.

God, the Son, is our Savior, as we can see in the earthly illustration below.

Imagine a single mother rabbit with four little bunnies beneath a porch. While she is out getting food for her family, the house and porch are on fire! How would the little bunnies know what to do? The bunnies are young, overwhelmed, and frozen in fear. The fire fighter has a hose in one hand and sees the little bunnies. He tells them to leave the area and flee for their life, however they don't understand and stay frozen in fear.

Finally, a bunny friend sees the situation, hurriedly hops over to the young bunnies, and convinces them, in their known bunny language, to flee. He waits for every bunny to leave the smoke-filled area. However, as he attempts to flee, the flames engulf the porch which collapses on him and he dies!

The bunny friend has sacrificed his life to show the young bunnies the way out of the burning fire. In the same way, Jesus, our Savior, saves us and gives us eternal life.

> *"For God so loved the world that he gave his one and only Son, that whoever believes in him shall not perish but have eternal life. For God did not send his Son into the world to condemn the world, but to save the world through him."* (John 3:16–17 NIV)

Jesus, God's only Son, is the Word who came to Earth in His human suit, the flesh, to save the world.

> *"He is dressed in a robe dipped in blood, and his name is the Word of God."* (Revelation 19:13 NIV)

> *"The Word became flesh and made his dwelling among us. We have seen his glory, the glory of the One and Only, who came from the Father, full of grace and truth."* (John 1:14 NIV)

Now let's dig into who God the Holy Spirit is.

Jesus gives us the Holy Spirit when we seek Him as our Savior so we can live this Christian life now in victory. The Holy Spirit lives within us and guides us in all wisdom.

> John the Baptist stated about Jesus: *"Then John gave this testimony: 'I saw the Spirit come down from heaven as a dove and remain on him. I would not have known him, except that the one who sent me to baptize with water told me,' 'The man on whom you see the Spirit come down and remain is he who will baptize with the Holy Spirit.' 'I have seen and I testify that this is the Son of God.'"* (John 1:32–34 NIV)

> *"While Apollos was at Corinth, Paul took the road through the interior and arrived at Ephesus. There he found some disciples and asked them, 'Did you receive the Holy Spirit when you believed?' They answered, 'No, we have not even heard that there is a Holy Spirit.' So Paul asked, 'Then what baptism did you receive?' 'John's baptism,' they replied. Paul said, 'John's baptism was a baptism of repentance. He told the people to believe in*

the one coming after him, that is, in Jesus.'
On hearing this, they were baptized into the
name of the Lord Jesus. When Paul placed his
hands on them, the Holy Spirit came on them,
and they spoke in tongues and prophesied."
(Acts 19:1–6 NIV)

Holy Spirit is my friend, guide and I am blessed God send Him to me in Jesus' name. He, the Holy Spirit is for you too—pray and seek Him, God wants you to have Him too!

When Jesus commissioned his disciples, He spoke of the Trinity:

"Therefore, go and make disciples of all
nations, baptizing them in the name of the
Father and of the Son and of the Holy Spirit,"
(Matthew 28:19 NIV)

And Apostle Paul in closing his letter to the Corinthian church also mentioned the Trinity.

"Finally, brothers and sisters, rejoice! Strive for
full restoration, encourage one another, be of
one mind, live in peace. And the God of love
and peace will be with you. Greet one another

> *with a holy kiss. All God's people here send*
> *their greetings. May the grace of the Lord*
> *Jesus Christ, and the love of God, and the*
> *fellowship of the Holy Spirit be with you all."*
> (2 Corinthians 13:11–14 NIV)

God the Father, God the Son, and God the Holy Spirit are one, yet have three different distinct roles and functions. Like your earthly Father has different roles as a son to his parents, an employee at work, friend, and so on.

REFLECTION

Take a walk outside and look at the leaves blowing in the wind. Do you feel God's presence? Where can you see God moving in your life?

God loved you so much that He sent his Son to be the ultimate sacrifice for you, to free you from sin and give you life eternal. How does that make you feel?

Have you received the Holy Spirit into your life? Recognize your need, pray, and trust that God hears your heart's desires. Receive the Holy Spirit in faith with praise and thanksgiving.

PRAYER

> *Lord, I thank you for sending your Son so I can have life eternal, be free from captivity and enjoy your daily blessings, with the wisdom and guidance I receive from the Holy Spirit. Thank you for these gifts you freely give, not because of the religious works I have done, but because you are a good, loving Father. In Jesus' name. Amen.*

Holy Spirit Truths

> *"But when he, the Spirit of truth, comes, he*
> *will guide you into all the truth. He will not*
> *speak on his own; he will speak only what he*
> *hears, and he will tell you what is yet to come."*
> (John 16:13 NIV)

TODAY'S INSPIRATION

Did you know that there is a person who is always truthful? This same person can lead you in all the ways of truth. When you desire change, hope, power, strength, and protection, this person is there. When you are confused about changes in your life, or if you can accomplish something, He is there. The person of the Holy Spirit is the one who does all this and so much more.

Who is this Holy Spirit? There can be some confusion about who He is. Simply, He is a person. He is the third person of the Trinity. God the Holy Spirit. **He is a spiritual person that comes to live inside of you and loves you.** He is also called the Spirit of Truth and the one that can be totally trusted with your life.

The Holy Spirit indwells you and joins you, the believer, to Jesus Christ and then He places you within the body of Christ among other believers to live for Him. While living in right relationship with the third person of the Godhead, the Holy Spirit, you live and fulfill your purpose on the Earth, free from sin.

How? The Holy Spirit unites the believer with Christ Jesus in His death so that all your old sinful ways die as Christ died. They are nailed to the cross with Jesus. Then, you are risen into a new life just as Christ was raised from the dead in His resurrection. From death to life eternal.

You have a new life in Christ when you submit your life to the control of the Holy Spirit and become victorious over sin just as Jesus was.

Let me share with you several things the Holy Spirit, the Spirit of Truth, does for and in you.

Hope. He is the way in which the God of hope fills you with joy as you trust Him. *"May the God of hope fill you with all joy and peace as you trust in him, so that* *you may overflow with hope by the power of the Holy Spirit."* (Romans 15:13 NIV)

Freedom. The Holy Spirit is not bound. Wherever He is, there is freedom and release from the chains of sin. *"Now the Lord is the Spirit, and where the Spirit of the Lord is, there is freedom."* (2 Corinthians 3:17 NIV)

Power. The Holy Spirit is the manifested power of God. When He comes upon your life you will live in power. *"But you will receive power when the Holy Spirit comes on you; and you will be my witnesses in Jerusalem, and in all Judea and Samaria, and to the ends of the earth."* (Acts 1:8 NIV)

Teacher. He will teach you anything you need to know. *"But the Counselor, the Holy Spirit, whom the Father will send in my name, will teach you all things and will remind you of everything I have said to you."* (John 14:26 NIV)

My life has drastically changed for the better since the Holy Spirit has made His home in me. Join me and make a point of getting to know this person, God the Holy Spirit.

REFLECTION

Think about how wonderful it would be to get to know a person that will never leave you, never forsake you, and is all the truth you will ever need. The person of the Holy Spirit is your best friend. He will help you understand the Bible and reveal Jesus to you. He is your protector and guide through life. He loves you deeply and helps you with all your life issues.

PRAYER

> *Holy Spirit, I desire truth, your truth in my life. Help me to know you and develop a friendship with you. Thank you for coming into my life, leading me, and teaching me who you and Jesus are so that I may welcome you both. Thank you for loving me completely. Help me to never ignore you but always be aware of your presence. In Jesus' name. Amen.*

The Gift of Tongues

"All of them were filled with the Holy Spirit and began to speak in other tongues as the Spirit enabled them." (Acts 2:4 NIV)

TODAY'S INSPIRATION

Speaking in tongues is a gift from God. Those that have received Jesus Christ as their Savior can receive this gift and enjoy its benefits.

When you pray in the Spirit, your spirit is speaking directly to God, who is Spirit. Scholars and clergymen refer to this as speaking in tongues, or an unknown language. It's like having a direct phone line connection to God. When you pray in the Spirit it is a language the devil cannot mess with. This prayer language is a secret weapon you can use against the enemy in your life.

Speaking in this unknown tongue is not something you conjure up, it is the Holy Spirit speaking to God, with your consent, as you move your mouth and tongue.

God's word teaches us that when you are filled with the Holy Spirit, you speak in other tongues as the Spirit of God gives utterance. Speaking in tongues is not the only evidence—or sign—of the baptism of the Holy Spirit, however it is important.

People in different walks of life have said, "Speaking in tongues was only for the original disciples." That is not true. Let me share with you what the Bible says about this wonderful gift in Acts 10:44–46 NIV. *"While Peter was still speaking these words, the Holy Spirit came on all who heard the message. The circumcised believers who had come with Peter were astonished that the gift of the Holy Spirit had been poured out even on Gentiles. For they heard them speaking in tongues and praising God."* (You can read the entire story in Acts 10:1–48.)

What a wonderful scene this must have been, the Holy Spirit fell on all who heard the words. Not some. ALL.

There may be times when you are not able to find the words in our human language. There are times when the heaviness of your trial may be too much to bear. That is the time when praying in tongues, through the Spirit, will help you. The Spirit helps you pray the perfect prayer when you cannot do it on your own.

Prayer usually starts out naturally and can happen anywhere. You may be thinking about work, food, chores, or problems, when the Holy Spirit nudges you to pray. Remember, this perfect gift from the Holy Spirit is there to help. As you pray in tongues, you will soon begin praying the glorious will of God. When you don't know what to pray, speak in tongues; it is always perfect.

God knows what you need in every situation. He has the perfect solution. You pray that perfect answer when you pray in tongues because it bypasses your mind and your will. You strengthen your faith when you pray in tongues, which is a great benefit to you and those you are praying for.

> *"But you, dear friends, build yourselves up in your most holy faith and pray in the Holy Spirit."* (Jude 1:20 NIV)

Desire the gift of tongues today. All you need to do is ask God in Jesus' name, have faith, and receive.

REFLECTION

How will you renew your prayer life and strengthen the practice with the gift of praying in tongues? The Holy Spirit wants to co-labor with you in prayer. His desire is that you pray His perfect, loving will. You may need to visit a spiritual leader or pastor and ask them to guide you. Seek the gift of speaking in tongues from God today.

PRAYER

> *Lord, I ask you to fill me with your presence and give me my heavenly language. I desire to speak with other tongues as the Spirit gives utterance to me. I thank you for this precious gift. In Jesus' name. Amen.*

Healing is a Promise

"*But he was wounded for our transgressions, he was bruised for our iniquities: the chastisement of our peace was upon him; and with his stripes we are healed.*" (Isaiah 53:5 KJV)

TODAY'S INSPIRATION

Jesus is good. Focus on those three words for a moment.

Know and believe that He is filled with goodness for you and for all humankind. Jesus is everything good and whole, therefore in Him is no sickness. Yet you may say, "there are still sick people," yes, there are. However, that doesn't mean that Jesus is not good. In Him is no sickness and He is called *Jehovah Rapha*, which means the "Lord God our Healer." You read of Jesus in the New Testament, "*How God anointed Jesus of Nazareth with the Holy Ghost and with power: who went about doing*

35

good and healing all that were oppressed of the devil; for God was with him." (Acts 10:38 KJV)

Jesus healed ALL who came to him. The Bible makes this clear. If you are sick, you can be comforted with the knowledge and promise that Jesus is still the healer today. "Jesus healed them all," is found repeatedly in the Bible.

Sickness is hard to endure. It causes our lives to be disrupted, and it fills our minds with fear. Jesus is not slack concerning His promises. He always accomplishes what His word says He will do. He never turned away a sick person.

God does not put sickness on anyone to teach them a lesson. You don't have to earn healing. Jesus never stopped healing people, past and present. Now, you, as a believer, can heal others and yourself in the name of Jesus, by the authority given to us by Him.

> *"And these signs will accompany those who believe: In my name they will drive out demons; they will speak in new tongues; they will pick up snakes with their hands; and when they drink deadly poison, it will not hurt them at all; they will place their hands on sick people, and they will get well."*
> (Mark 16:17–18 NIV)

It may be difficult for the human brain to comprehend that you can heal just as Jesus used his power. In fact, the Bible says you are to do even greater things because Jesus ascended to the Father. Believe with faith The Word of all Truths.

Imagine: power to raise the dead, heal the sick, and cast out demons. That power is in you through the Holy Spirit. It is the same power that raised Jesus from the dead.

> *"And if the Spirit of him who raised Jesus from the dead is living in you, he who raised Christ from the dead will also give life to your mortal bodies through his Spirit who lives in you."*
> (Romans 8:11 NIV)

No matter what you are going through, you can trust and believe that what you ask for in prayer, you will receive it in Jesus' name. Pray over your own body. Pray over your family. Pray over others. Trust God's promises, they never fail.

> *"For no matter how many promises God has made, they are "Yes" in Christ. And so through him "Amen" is spoken by us to the glory of God."* (2 Corinthians 1:20 NIV)

REFLECTION

Are you sick today? Jesus is the healer. Ponder in your heart what it will be like to be well and whole in your body. God is for you and His promises are a yes, as you say "Amen." Think about these things; imagine what you will do after you are healthy. Allow these ideas to motivate you to put your complete faith in God for healing.

PRAYER

> *Lord, thank you for sending your son to take all sin and sickness upon himself so we can be free and no longer captives. I am healed from the top of my head to the tip of my toes, by the blood of Jesus. By the stripes you took on your body, I claim my healing now and give glory to my Father in Heaven. In Jesus' name. Amen.*

The Power of The Word

"He was in the world, and though the world was made through him, the world did not recognize him." (John 1:10 NIV)

TODAY'S INSPIRATION

Has anyone said a word to you that has not left your mind?

I remember a time when words stung me as a peer was making fun of my 4th grade self. It was two words: Pizza Face. I write about healing from hurtful bullying and other past events in my memoir, *Change Course*. It is a story of healing by the grace of God.

The power of words is clearly shown in the bible from the beginning when God created the world. Genesis 1:3, 6, 9, 11, 14, 20, 24, and verse 26. God said and spoke into existence light, sky, land, vegetation, sun, moon, stars, birds, sea creatures and every living thing in the water, land, and sky. Wild animals, livestock, and lastly God made us, humankind in His image.

Repeatedly, the bible verses begin with "God said . . ." With words God spoke life into existence. When we read deeper into the bible, we discover that when God spoke it was Jesus, the Word, who created everything. Nothing exists that was not created through Jesus.

> *"In the beginning was the Word, and the Word*
> *was with God, and the Word was God. He*
> *was with God in the beginning. Through him*
> *all things were made;"* (John 1:1–3a NIV)

In revelation 19:13 NIV when John speaks of Jesus, he clarifies who The Word is: *"He is dressed in a robe dipped in blood, and his name is the Word of God."*

God wanted to have an intimate relationship with us and save the word from sin, so He sent The Word, Jesus. In the bible there is much about the ministry of Jesus in the flesh, we will not touch on it all in this devotion, however I do want to discuss the power of The Word further.

To demonstrate how powerful The Word is let's look at an example of how to walk on water.

*"Shortly before dawn Jesus went out to them,
walking on the lake. When the disciples saw
him walking on the lake, they were terrified.
'It's a ghost,' they said, and cried out in fear. But
Jesus immediately said to them: 'Take cour-
age! It is I. Don't be afraid.' 'Lord, if it's you,'
Peter replied, 'tell me to come to you on the
water.' 'Come,' he said. Then Peter got down
out of the boat, walked on the water, and came
toward Jesus. But when he saw the wind, he
was afraid and, beginning to sink, cried out,
'Lord, save me!' Immediately, Jesus reached out
his hand and caught him. 'You of little faith,'
he said, 'why did you doubt?' And when they
climbed into the boat, the wind died down.
Then those who were in the boat worshiped
him, saying, 'Truly you are the Son of God.'"*
(Matthew 14:25–33 NIV)

When Jesus said "come," that word had the power
to allow Peter to walk on water. The problem came in
when Peter doubted. If we listen and believe The Words
spoken by Jesus without doubt, we can move mountains.

*"He replied, Because you have so little faith. I
tell you the truth, if you have faith as small*

> *as a mustard seed, you can say to this moun-*
> *tain, 'Move from here to there' and it will*
> *move. Nothing will be impossible for you."*
> (Matthew 17:20–21 NIV)

Speak to your mountains, your problems, in faith and see them move in Jesus' name!

REFLECTION

Why do you think God called Jesus, The Word?

Do you speak life and encouragement to others?

Have you heard any words of discouragement spoken against you which need to be released? Give those hurtful words to Jesus and never think of them again.

PRAYER

> *Heavenly Father, I thank you for sending*
> *Jesus, The Word, because you love us and want*
> *to give us eternal life through Him. Help us*
> *understand the power of The Word in our*
> *daily lives and speak only life, and love into*
> *others. In Jesus' name. Amen.*

Jesus the Healer

"He himself bore our sins in his body on the tree, so that we might die to sins and live for righteousness; by his wounds you have been healed." (I Peter 2:24 NIV)

TODAY'S INSPIRATION

Pain is a great indicator that something is wrong. When we have a pain or sickness in our bodies, we tend to focus on that. It usually gets our attention and disrupts our day and schedules. The Lord wants you to focus on something else. Instead, focus on the promises in His word concerning healing.

Today's scripture above tells us that Jesus bore our sin in His body. He also took sicknesses into His body, because of the beating, the stripes, Jesus took for us, we are healed today. This is a great promise to stand on.

Notice the words "you have been healed." This is past tense, meaning you are healed right now. You are healed through Jesus as you grow your understanding of what He has already done for you. Manifest your healing now, it is finished, Jesus already paid the ultimate price by the beatings and stripes He endured for your healing and wholeness.

If you need a healing, find a quiet place to sit alone with Jesus and focus your mind on what He has done for you in His body. Take time to quiet your soul and connect with the Holy Spirit in worship. Thank Jesus for healing you and that you receive your healing now.

See that sickness or problem leaving your body. Allow the presence of Jesus to wash over you as He takes it away. Focus on the healer, Jesus, healing you in this moment of cancers, colds, heart issues, depression, and more. Nothing is too big for Him; nothing is larger than the name of Jesus Christ. Receive your promise today.

Imagine and see yourself healed and see that sickness, that thing, shrinking and gone from your life today. Make the confession every day that by His stripes, you are healed. Stand firm and believe.

Thank Jesus and tell Him how much you appreciate Him for your healing and returning you to wholeness.

Sense the peace flood through your body as it is being restored to full health because of the Holy Spirit's power with the mind of Jesus within you.

Thank Jesus now with worship and praise for His sacrifice that has given you these healings.

I encourage you do to this often, even daily, to maintain your health and live a life pro-actively walking in healing.

REFLECTION

Take some time and reflect on what your body and life look like as you walk in the glorious Kingdom of health. What does your life look like fully restored? What will you do? Jesus is a friend to you and wants you well. Think about and ponder in your heart that the sickness is no longer yours. It is His. Give it to Jesus today. He is big enough, mighty enough, strong enough to handle it all. Hold nothing back.

Seek Jesus' will for your life and imagine the places you will go. Why imagine this? Because if you can see yourself doing it, you will do it.

The Lord Jesus Christ is your healer with the power of the Holy Spirit in you. His love for you is personal. Feel Him wrapping His loving, healing arms around you right now. He desires you well and healthy to do His will on the Earth.

PRAYER

> *Lord, I thank you so much for healing my body
> and for what you took in Your body for me. I
> thank you for taking all my sickness and dis-
> ease into yourself. You have brought me to a
> place of healing and wholeness. I am healed
> and gratefully walk in divine healing every
> day. Keep my body strong and guide me to
> live out your purpose for me on the earth. In
> Jesus' name. Amen.*

Our Authority

"I have given you authority to trample on snakes and scorpions and to overcome all the power of the enemy; nothing will harm you. However, do not rejoice that the spirits submit to you, but rejoice that your names are written in heaven." (Luke 10:19–20 NIV)

TODAY'S INSPIRATION

Jesus has all authority, because of His obedience to the Father. Jesus, in turn, gives that authority to those who believe and follow Him in obedience.

God has given you and me this authority because of Jesus' victory on the cross. We live in a fallen world (see Genesis 3). Satan is in this world system and will try to attack us. Jesus gave us authority over the enemy while we are here.

We must constantly take our authority Jesus has given us and walk in it. You must know first your authority through Jesus and then declare it by the blood of Jesus that has been shed for you and me. Know and declare! Conquer and have victory!

Imagine a bank robber trying to rob a bank. He tries even though he does not have the authority to steal the money. Satan is like that bank robber. He tries—even though he does not have the authority—to steal your health, joy, prosperity, or anything else. Do not let him win, YOU are victorious through Jesus!

When you comprehend what Jesus has done for you concerning the authority you have, the challenges and difficulties of life will never defeat you. We are not called to live a life free of challenges. We are called to have authority over them.

How do you walk in this authority? You walk by faith with Jesus.

Faith deals with what is in the unseen realm. If you can see it in the natural, you don't need faith. You must believe that you walk in victory before you may visually see the results in the natural because of your authority given to you by Jesus.

> *"The God who gives life to the dead and calls into being things that were not."* (Romans 4:17b NIV)

We are to resist the sins, passions, and evil desires which the devil tries to put on us in our mind. The devil wants you to believe the lies that he brings. Moreover, you are to tell the devil and his little demons, "NO" in Jesus' name, and take authority over those thoughts.

When the enemy comes with feelings of anger, jealousy, pride, depression, loneliness, or fear, you are to take authority over those feelings and give them no place in your heart or mind. Do not entertain the enemy in any area. Instead, read a scripture, and meditate on it. Speak it out loud over and over so your mind can hear it and drown out the evil thoughts. The word of God has given me comfort many times.

One night about six months ago I was in bed and I saw a demon jump on me and try to pester me. I took my bible laid it on my chest and repeatedly spoke God's word, with authority, and the loser, the demon, eventually left me alone.

> *"Submit yourselves, then, to God. Resist the devil, and he will flee from you."* (James 4:7 NIV)

Speak the word of God in your life and bring new power to your situations and thoughts.

When sickness, disease, pain, or weakness come on your body, keep declaring that "by the stripes of Jesus

I am healed." State emphatically what the word says as you reclaim your authority over your life in Jesus' name. Declare with your mouth, believe in your mind and soul that you have freedom from these things and that you are free by Jesus Christ's blood.

REFLECTION

Make a list of things that you know you need to have authority over in your life. Where are you letting the enemy have control? Take that authority back today as you speak with your mouth what you know to be true from the word of God. Do not let your authority lie dormant, reclaim control.

Jesus has given you the authority over all the power of the enemy. Use it today and don't be shy!

PRAYER

> *Lord, I thank you for the authority I can walk in, and that you wrote my name in heaven. Help me live in this authority every day. I ask you to help me remember to walk in what you have already provided, and that I will take hold—together with you—in all of life's problems and situations. In Jesus' name. Amen.*

Miracles and Blessings

"'The Spirit of the Lord is on me, because he
has anointed me to preach good news to the
poor. He has sent me to proclaim freedom for
the prisoners and recovery of sight for the blind,
to release the oppressed, to proclaim the year
of the Lord's favor.' Then he rolled up the scroll,
gave it back to the attendant and sat down.
The eyes of everyone in the synagogue were
fastened on him, and he began by saying to
them, 'Today this scripture is fulfilled in your
hearing.'" (Luke 4:18–21 NIV)

TODAY'S INSPIRATION

Miracles and blessings are wonderful and bring us joy
each and every time they happen. I have been healed
instantly in my body twice by a ball of light and pain

has instantly left my body in the Name of Jesus countless times (I call them miracles). Also, I have been healed over a period of time of a variety of ailments (I call them blessings). Healings and blessings don't come the same way every time.

I love today's verse because it tells us what Jesus came to do. The verse is His purpose statement in the Earth and the purpose of His ministry.

Recently, I attended two church services and then ministered to the poor all in one day. I was blessed to interact with other Christians and the homeless in a loving way. When the day was over, I had a terrible back pain. I didn't do any strenuous work, yet my back was feeling a lot of pain.

As I lay in bed that night with this back pain, I asked my husband to pray for me. He stopped quietly speaking in tongues, placed his hands on me, and then continued praying. Instantly, my soul did a little dance, and the pain left my body. It was a miracle as Jesus flowed through my husband's hands into my back, and I was healed. Thank you, Jesus!

When I was 52, I was hemorrhaging for a couple of weeks and in the middle of the night as I lay in bed, my heart began to beat extremely fast and woke me up. Just then a bright ball of light came to me from across the room and instantly healed me. What an amazing miracle! Then our loving God did it again and healed me from severe cold and flu like symptoms with another ball of light just two weeks after the first ball of light miracle.

Sometimes healing comes through instructions the Holy Spirit gives us about what we should do for our bodies. For example, a change in our food choices or avoiding detrimental activities.

Because Jesus is so faithful, we can pray for ourselves by laying hands on our own body and He will heal us. He loves you so much and is here for you. Trust and believe in His miracle working power in your life today.

REFLECTION

Take time today and reflect on the many blessings of the Lord and how you have been blessed with healing in your body. Has the Lord miraculously saved you, healed you, protected you? Thank Him for those things.

Sometimes we are our own worst enemy and do not take care of the glorious body God has given us. Seek Holy Spirit for guidance and make any needed changes so your body functions in kingdom health here on Earth.

Make time to thank Jesus for His goodness and reflect on all that He has done for you.

PRAYER

> *Lord, thank you for your many blessings, miracles, and many ways of protection over my body. Thank you for loving me so much today. I thank you for the blessings, good health, peace, and prosperity today. I ask you to continue to show me ways to make good choices and cooperate with healings in my body. In Jesus' name. Amen.*

Joy Always

"*May the God of hope fill you with all joy and peace as you trust in Him, so that you may overflow with hope by the power of the Holy Spirit.*" (Romans 15:13 NIV)

TODAY'S INSPIRATION

The fruit of joy is an incredible gift that the Holy Spirit gives us. Joy is one of the fruits of the Holy Spirit. Today's verse tells us that God fills you with joy and peace. Why does God want you to have joy? Because the verse says, "So that you will overflows with hope."

Why do you need hope? Because we live in a world where hope can be in short supply. Some people are hopeless right now, yet, hope is the anchor of faith. Hope begins the process and then it manifests faith in the present. You are meant to overflow, to enjoy more than enough, so much so that you can't contain it. Joy gets rid of the negativity in your life and from around you. You don't have to strive for joy. You don't have to work for joy. Jesus freely fills you with joy as you pray and worship Him.

When you are at peace, joy will rise naturally. Most people think that joy is happiness, however joy is different. Joy is strength when you face trouble. Joy is strength to go through a situation. When you are full of joy in the Lord, you won't have to fear the circumstances that fill your mind. You will stand under the pressure of what comes and have victory in Jesus.

When you have a dark night of the soul or a season of sadness, you need to use your joy. When you feel weak and defeated, you need to access your joy in the Lord.

Joy is not dependent on your circumstances. Joy comes from the knowledge you have of Jesus, knowing that He is for you and with you always. Joy is always there because joy is found in Jesus. Don't think that all your circumstances must change before you have joy. You can walk in joy right now no matter what your situation looks like.

Allow joy to overwhelm your situations. Allow joy to speak through your circumstances.

Be still in your soul and know that Jesus is for you.

Make joy a personal pursuit because joy is always around. Don't wait to feel better to feel the joy. Claim it now.

Jesus shed His blood so we can have victory now, for all eternity and be full of joy and peace. Don't give up your joy to the enemy, call upon Jesus anytime to remain in joy and leave no room for the joy to be lost in your life.

REFLECTION

When is the last time you really felt the joy of the Lord? Ponder this for a few minutes. When you felt joy, relish in your strength and ability to conquer anything that came at you. You felt stronger because joy is a building block to help you overcome challenges.

What would happen if you always walked in joy? Imagine how your circumstances would be victorious in the Lord.

Think about two areas of your life where you need more joy. Determine how you can channel joy no matter what comes your way.

PRAYER

> *Lord, help me embrace your joy and let it over-*
> *flow in me every day. Let me be a conduit for*
> *your joy and show that to the world. Help me*
> *not to worry about situations and allow them*
> *to overcome my mood. Let joy and peace fill me,*
> *so that I see your strength in my life. Let hope*
> *rise and overflow in me. In Jesus' name. Amen.*

Love Walk

"*Love is patient, love is kind. It does not envy, it does not boast, it is not proud. It is not rude, it is not self-seeking, it is not easily angered, it keeps no record of wrongs. Love does not delight in evil but rejoices with the truth. It always protects, always trusts, always hopes, always perseveres.*" (1 Corinthians 13:4–7 NIV)

TODAY'S INSPIRATION

Your love walk with Jesus is unique in that Jesus loves you like you are the only one to love.

Ponder and wonder about the powerful verse above, and how the Bible tells us exactly what love is to be like. Walking in love will bring light upon your path and in your relationship with Jesus so you can see a victory in trials you have. Read the verse again very slowly. Then ask yourself: *What is love? How have I experienced love in a healthy way?*

Earthly love is alive as Jesus commanded us to love one another, yet it is worldly flawed and has boundaries. Still, we must seek to love others as Jesus loves us.

We can only attribute limitless and without boundaries love to one person. Who you ask? His name is Jesus.

In the Bible, it says that love covers a multitude of sins. If you are like me, I am not perfect, as hard as I try to be. Thankfully, Jesus' loves us in the midst of sin.

> *"Above all, love each other deeply, because*
> *love covers over a multitude of sins."*
> (1 Peter 4:8 NIV)

Who can tell how many sins are in a multitude? Generally, in this context, "multitude," refers to more sins than you can name. Think of it—real, genuine love will cover, hide, and put out of sight more sins than you can name. He will cover them. That is such glorious, good news.

> *"But God demonstrates his own love for us in*
> *this: While we were still sinners, Christ died*
> *for us."* (Romans 5:8 NIV)

Jesus Christ died for your sins so they could be covered by His love. His love buries your sins. They are gone because of His love. When He says sins are covered and hidden, this means God, you and others cannot see them any longer, Hallelujah!

Love is the most powerful force on the Earth. When you walk in love with Jesus, this means you do not criticize, judge, or condemn others, no matter what they have done. Each of us is to be responsible for confessing and repenting our sins before God.

> *"Love does not delight in evil but rejoices with the truth. It always protects, always trusts, always hopes, always perseveres."*
> (1 Corinthians 13:6–7 NIV)

Believe and receive by faith that Jesus has purchased for you salvation so you can be free of sin, healing, and fullness of the Spirit, grace, mercy, peace, joy and all the fruit of the Spirit. He has also shed His love in your heart.

> *"Love must be sincere. Hate what is evil; cling to what is good."* (Romans 12:9 NIV)

Love trumps hate and evil. Love everyone that you meet. When you do this, all men will know that you belong to God and that you walk with Him.

Jesus loves you. Receive Him today and walk in love.

REFLECTION

Love is a beautiful word and being loved is a wonderful feeling. When you think about love, what comes to mind? How do you feel? What does Jesus loving you mean to you? Are you walking with Him in love?

PRAYER

> *Lord, thank you for your love for all your children, including me. Thank you for loving all of humankind and helping me to walk with you every day. Lord, thank you for covering all my sins and loving me unconditionally. I ask you, Lord, to help me love others the way you love me. Thank you. In Jesus' name. Amen.*

Why the Cross

"In Him we have redemption through his blood,
the forgiveness of sins, in accordance with the
riches of God's grace." (Ephesians 1:7 NIV)

TODAY'S INSPIRATION

When you read about Law in the Old Testament, you find that God created legal rulings and moral injunctions so people would have direction and understand right from wrong. The laws of sacrifice didn't take away their sins for all eternity but was a foreshadowing of Jesus. The Old Testament scriptures pointed to Jesus, yet people didn't fully realize these implications during this period of time.

In the verses below Paul refers to the Old Testament legal requirements calling them a "shadow of things to come." Paul did not speak against the Law but rather spoke of Jesus as superior to this Law.

> *"Therefore do not let anyone judge you by what*
> *you eat or drink, or with regard to a religious*
> *festival, a New Moon celebration or a Sabbath*
> *day."* (Colossians 2:16 NIV)

> *"These are a shadow of the things that were to*
> *come; the reality, however, is found in Christ."*
> (Colossians 2:17 NIV)

There are man's laws and God's laws, and both have consequences to breaking those laws.

When you break a law, you pay a consequence for breaking it, if caught. You may get a warning, pay a fine, or go to jail, or worse, depending on what you did.

Before Jesus Christ, the Jewish people were in God's old covenant. Consider that before Jesus came and shed His blood for our sins, people had to handle sin based on scripture in the Old Testament.

> *"Moses took half of the blood and put it in bowls,*
> *and the other half he splashed against the*
> *altar. Then he took the Book of the Covenant*
> *and read it to the people. They responded, 'We*
> *will do everything the LORD has said; we*
> *will obey.' Moses then took the blood, sprinkled*
> *it on the people and said, 'This is the blood*

*of the covenant that the LORD has made
with you in accordance with all these words.'"*
(Exodus 24:6–8 NIV)

Prior to Jesus' death and resurrection, atonement, reconciliation of God and humankind, was primarily possible by sacrificing animals in the Temple.

God's old covenant laws required offering animal's blood as a sacrifice for the forgiveness of sins. Jesus died on the cross once so we would no longer need to kill animals continually for blood sacrifices and the forgiveness of our sins. Jesus made atonement, amends, for humans once and for all so we could be righteous before God. Because of His blood sacrifice, we all are holy and set apart for Him, forever, starting when we receive Jesus into your heart.

We don't need to offer sacrifices to atone for our sins. There is a better way, a more perfect way and Jesus' blood provides that way.

Jesus Christ's blood paid the price for all our sins, past, present and those in our future. He took care of all sins, forever.

*"The Holy Spirit also testifies to us about this.
First he says: 'This is the covenant I will make
with them after that time, says the Lord. I*

> *will put my laws in their hearts, and I will*
> *write them on their minds.' Then he adds:*
> *'Their sins and lawless acts I will remem-*
> *ber no more.' And where these have been for-*
> *given, sacrifice for sin is no longer necessary."*
> (Hebrews 10:15–18 NIV)

To partake of this sacrifice and forgiveness of our sins, all you need to do is accept the way of the cross. If you have not repented of your sins and received Jesus Christ as your Savior, you can do so at the end of today's devotion. In addition, there is a Salvation prayer at the end of this book.

REFLECTION

This is a sacred moment. If you have never asked the Lord Jesus to be your Savior, you can do so now. If you need to repent of any sin and get forgiveness through His blood you can do so now. Read the following scripture and confess, believe, and receive Jesus Christ as your personal Savior. Confess Him to be Lord and believe in your heart that God raised Jesus from the dead. This is all you need to do. Believe that He shed His blood for you, so you won't be lost forever.

"That if you confess with your mouth the Lord Jesus and believe in your heart that God has raised Him from the dead, you will be saved. For with the heart one believes unto righteousness, and with the mouth confession is made unto salvation. For the Scripture says, 'Whoever believes on Him will not be put to shame.' For there is no distinction between Jew and Greek, for the same Lord over all is rich to all who call upon Him. For 'whoever calls on the name of the Lord shall be saved.'"
(Romans 10:9–13 KJV)

PRAYER

Lord, thank you for saving me by your sacrifice on the cross. Thank you for accepting me as your child and for your forgiveness of all my sins. I repent today of all my sins and receive and accept you as my Lord and Savior. In Jesus' name. Amen.

God is Good

> *"And he passed in front of Moses, proclaiming, 'The Lord, the Lord, the compassionate and gracious God, slow to anger, abounding in love and faithfulness.'"* (Exodus 34:6 NIV)

TODAY'S INSPIRATION

A positive relationship with our good God comes out of knowing His nature and His real character which is superior goodness all the time.

In the Old Testament, before Jesus walked the Earth as a man, God had to give laws and enforce them with punishment, sometimes even severe penalties, to deter the people from sin.

If you have young children, you likely will relate to this while raising them. There are times when—because they lack experience and understanding—it may not be possible to reason with them. For example, you may find it difficult to tell them in a way they will understand why they should share, take turns, why they should not be selfish, or refrain from taking items away from others.

Your children may not understand the concepts of their actions. If they repeat a wrong action, they will be punished. To discipline is to teach them and to protect them.

God loves you and me, and while we were sinners, Christ died for us. The New Testament teaches us that God extends His love to us while we are living in sin, not after we have gotten our lives right and come to Him. We receive the love even if we are not perfect and righteous.

A great example of how much Jesus loves us is when a woman was found in adultery and brought to Jesus.

> John 8:3–11 NIV says: *"The teachers of the law and the Pharisees brought in a woman caught in adultery. They made her stand before the group and said to Jesus, 'Teacher, this woman was caught in the act of adultery. In the Law, Moses commanded us to stone such women. Now, what do you say?' They were using this question as a trap, to have a basis for*

accusing him. But Jesus bent down and started to write on the ground with his finger. When they kept on questioning him, he straightened up and said to them, 'If any one of you is without sin, let him be the first to throw a stone at her.' Again, he stooped down and wrote on the ground. At this, those who heard began to go away one at a time, the older ones first, until only Jesus was left, with the woman still standing there. Jesus straightened up and asked her, 'Woman, where are they? Has no one condemned you?' 'No one, sir,' she said. 'Then neither do I condemn you,' Jesus declared. 'Go now and leave your life of sin.'"

Wow! She didn't ask for Him to love her or forgive her; it was freely given. She was able to be free of sin because of the goodness of God and go on to lead a better life, and so can you.

REFLECTION

Think of a time that God was good to you, but you perceived you didn't deserve His goodness. When you knew you missed His desires for you by a mile, yet realized He was good to you, what did you do? Think about why He was so good to you in the situation. He was good because He loved you. Think on that love for a minute and rejoice in that.

PRAYER

> *Lord, I thank you for being so good to me. Thank you for loving me when I believed I didn't deserve love and for being good to me without me having to earn your goodness. I love you and I ask you to grow my roots deep down into your love for me. Help me to be your hand extended to love others, as you have loved me. In Jesus' name. Amen.*

Grace

> "For the grace of God has appeared that offers
> salvation to all people. It teaches us to say 'No'
> to ungodliness and worldly passions, and to
> live self-controlled, upright and godly lives in
> this present age." (Titus 2:11–12 NIV)

TODAY'S INSPIRATION

The empowering presence of God that comes to you
in your life is grace that enables you to do what you
thought you couldn't do in the flesh. Grace helps you
to believe what you can't believe, helps you to do the
impossible and believe the impossible. Grace is free, not
an earned favor.

With God's grace there is nothing you cannot do, or
achieve, in Him and with Him. What has been done

on the cross 2,000 years ago was by grace and can be accessed by faith in our lives right now.

> *"When you were dead in your sins and in the uncircumcision of your sinful nature, God made you alive with Christ. He forgave us all our sins, having canceled the written code, with its regulations, that was against us and that stood opposed to us; he took it away, nailing it to the cross. And having disarmed the powers and authorities, he made a public spectacle of them, triumphing over them by the cross."* (Colossians 2:13–15 NIV)

Before you were born, God took care of the devil and his works. By His grace, Jesus made an open display and shame of him on the cross and rendered the devil powerless. Did you know that God's grace has a past, a present, and a future? All three dimensions are for you!

God's grace, love and mercy went to work for you before you were born; this is the "Past Tense" of grace. Before time and creation, God was looking ahead to your glorious "expected end!" Let's investigate the Old Testament when Jeremiah the prophet sent a letter to elders, captives, priests, prophets, and to many others, (including you. Insert yourself into bible stories because God's Word is alive and active) and see how God has been thinking about you.

> *"'For I know the plans I have for you,' declares the LORD, 'plans to prosper you and not to harm you, plans to give you hope and a future. Then you will call on me and come and pray to me, and I will listen to you. You will seek me and find me when you seek me with all your heart. I will be found by you,' declares the LORD,"* (Jeremiah 29:11–14a NIV)

Through Jesus' death on the cross, we are free of guilt or sin. Justification of life has come upon all people. You may enter the grace that was provided before the world began. This again shows Past Tense Grace that you obtain now in the Present Tense.

> *"And are justified freely by his grace through the redemption that came by Christ Jesus. God presented him as a sacrifice of atonement, through faith in his blood. He did this to demonstrate his justice, because in his forbearance he had left the sins committed beforehand unpunished—he did it to demonstrate*

*his justice at the present time, so as to be just
and the one who justifies those who have faith
in Jesus."* (Romans 3:24–26 NIV)

His Present Grace is His provision and strength for every need you have today. It is the raw material from which you can, by faith, enter salvation and construct a victorious life.

Apostle Paul: *"Three times I pleaded with the Lord to take it away from me. But he said to me, 'My grace is sufficient for you, for my power is made perfect in weakness.' Therefore, I will boast all the more gladly about my weaknesses, so that Christ's power may rest on me. That is why, for Christ's sake, I delight in weaknesses, in insults, in hardships, in persecutions, in difficulties. For when I am weak, then I am strong."*
(2 Corinthians 12:8–10 NIV)

There is a Future Dimension to God's grace. The coming of the Lord is the beginning of "future grace."

"'Men of Galilee,' they said, 'why do you stand here looking into the sky? This same Jesus, who

*has been taken from you into heaven, will
come back in the same way you have seen him
go into heaven.'"* (Acts 1:11 NIV)

REFLECTION

Think about the ways grace has empowered you in your life and thank Jesus.

Look at other areas in your life where you desire His power to make it a reality in this earthly realm. Consider when you need grace, and favor will be given freely to you as you seek Him.

PRAYER

God, your grace is so wonderful in my life. I thank you so much for it. I ask you to give me more grace and help me grow in grace. Thank you for loving me and thinking of me before the world began. I ask you for your help to do the impossible in my life by your grace. In Jesus' name. Amen.

Faith Victory

". . . for everyone born of God overcomes the world. This is the victory that has overcome the world, even our faith." (I John 5:4 NIV)

TODAY'S INSPIRATION

Faith speaks and says, "It is mine NOW!" You don't have to see it to believe you have it. You can know you have it without seeing it by faith. Know you have what you asked for even if it doesn't show up today in the natural. You will achieve victory in your faith.

Hope says, "I will get what is mine one day." Faith says, "This is mine now!" Anything that points to the future is hope and not faith. That may be a shocking statement. Think about the differences between hope and faith.

Start believing with "right now" faith and you will receive your desires as they align with God's will.

> *"Now faith is confidence in what we hope for*
> *and assurance about what we do not see."*
> (Hebrews 11:1 NIV)

Really believe with your heart and imagination. Hold fast, do not give up. Believe and you will receive.

The word of God tells us *". . . hold firmly to the word of life."* (Philippians 2:16a NIV)

If you desire to grow your faith, here are some tips:

- Read God's word every day. Faith to believe and have a close relationship with Jesus will come from the word of God itself.
- Imagine yourself inside the word, living the promises out here and now.
- Believe God's word. You can't have faith in something if you don't believe it with your heart and mind.
- Praise God for the word of God. It is precious and you should hold it dear as necessary food for life.

Faith is more important than what we see with the natural eye. The spiritual realm is where faith resides and lives for all eternity. We need to learn how to take and receive from this heavenly spiritual dimension into our everyday natural environment so we can live Heaven on Earth and forever. Faith brings what is reality in the heavenlies, into the physical world.

The Bible talks about what is not seen as eternal and what you can see with your natural eyes as temporary.

> *"So we fix our eyes not on what is seen, but on what is unseen, since what is seen is temporary, but what is unseen is eternal."*
> (2 Corinthians 4:18 NIV)

To build yourself up and become confident in your faith, you first should begin with prayer. Find prayers in God's word and make them your own because His word is alive, active, and for all. (For an example, see Ephesians 3:14–21, a prayer for spiritual strength.)

Begin to pray for the will of God to be done in your life as it is in Heaven. Pray that you are rooted and established in love. Pray that the kingdom of God comes into your life just like it is in Heaven as you grow your roots deep within Jesus.

God wants to reveal the unseen realm into your seen realm. Everything you need that Jesus bought and paid for is in the heavenly realm. How do you access everything you need to live on Earth as it is in Heaven? By faith.

Faith is your currency, your purchasing power that Jesus freely gives to you because He has already purchased it with His blood.

Your faith can change the atmosphere; therefore, choose victory faith now, through Jesus, here and now on Earth and for all eternity in Heaven. Jesus paid the price to set all the captives free, which includes you and me. Jesus' work on the cross is finished. He is resurrected and our sins are fully paid for. Hallelujah!

> *"But thanks be to God! He gives us the victory through our Lord Jesus Christ."*
> (1 Corinthians 15:57 NIV)

REFLECTION

What do you need to pray for? Consider something that is in the heavenly realm that you need in the physical realm. Faith will get that into the visible realm.

Imagine what you are asking for, have faith for it, and praise God for His revealing process. The smallest faith reveals much. Spend time in prayer asking Him to show you His will in Heaven, and how to bring that to the Earth realm today. Imagine your heart's desire.

PRAYER

> *Lord, help any unbelief I have. Draw it out of me. Help me to see what I believe with the eyes of faith and to believe I have it right now. I pray for spiritual strength to see what I cannot see with my natural eyes and to see in my heart as you see. Help me to walk before you full of faith and belief. In Jesus' name. Amen.*

Greater Things

Jesus said: *"Verily, verily, I say unto you, He that believeth on me, the works that I do shall he do also; and greater works than these shall he do; because I go unto my Father."*
(John 14:12 KJV)

TODAY'S INSPIRATION

Today's verse is a powerful promise for you as a believer. If you have ever wondered if God could use you right now to make a difference in the world, He can. Jesus repeated the words "Verily, verily" in this verse to emphasis and let us know that we will do the same works He did here on the earth. Even far better, greater work, than He did.

Now, I have discovered what the "greater works" is, salvation! Jesus is the Savior and salvation is the ultimate work He wants us to tell others about. Jesus could not at that time offer the salvation we receive through the cross because He had not yet finished what He was sent to accomplish. He has now completed His work here on the Earth so we can benefit from salvation and more. We need to share this good news with others!

How do we share the salvation message? We allow Holy Spirit power to move and work through us to do what He wants to do on the Earth.

> *"When he had received the drink, Jesus said, 'It is finished.' With that, he bowed his head and gave up his spirit."* (John 19:30 NIV)

Now that Jesus' work is finished, He sent the Holy Spirit to accomplish greater work through us as we preach the Gospel, with signs and wonders following. Signs and wonders are good; however, the greatest thing is salvation. It is freely given to all! Spread the word!

The mighty work of Jesus and greater works would not be possible without Holy Spirit. He is your guide, He is your wisdom, He is your joy that overflows and fulfills the greater works around you by using your hands and feet here on Earth for His glory.

You don't have to wait for your life to be perfect before God uses you as a conduit to share the

Good News. There are people waiting for your gift to be released to them. They are waiting to be set free from their bondages. You are the key to their salvation when you, as a Christian, are filled with Holy Spirit power.

Christianity is built on God's love for you and thank goodness His Love covers our multitude of sins. Love is the most powerful force on the Earth and with our roots deep into Jesus' love we receive forgiveness by faith because of the finished work of Jesus Christ.

Step out today and give Jesus to the world any way you can. Offer a hug, a smile, a helping hand, or anything that demonstrates the love of Jesus.

Get rooted in Jesus and the Bible. Give the truth of Jesus, and the truth of your personal salvation, your testimony, to a "lost" friend you have, a store clerk or neighbor. You will be amazed at what Jesus will do through you.

REFLECTION

Have you ever thought about what God wants to do through you? God is about saving the souls of people and wanting them to know Him intimately.

Pray right now and ask Him how you can be Jesus' hands and feet today. Write down what comes to you, meditate, give thanks, then go and do!

PRAYER

Lord, use my life for your greater works. Show me what I can do on the Earth to glorify you and share your salvation message. Help me to partner with you to save the lost. Help me to yield to you and not be afraid of what can be done through me. With you, I have power. In Jesus' name. Amen.

Signs and Wonders

"*And these signs shall follow them that believe;
In my name shall they cast out devils; they
shall speak with new tongues; They shall take
up serpents; and if they drink any deadly
thing, it shall not hurt them; they shall lay
hands on the sick, and they shall recover.*"
(Mark 16:17–18 KJV)

TODAY'S INSPIRATION

We may not think much about signs and wonders in our
life; however, they are all around us. The Bible says that
signs and wonders follow those that believe.

What exactly are signs and wonders? They refer to
experiences that are perceived to be miraculous and
almost unexplainable in the life of a person that is a

Christian or non-Christian. They are considered as being normative in the modern Christian experience.

The verse above says that these types of experiences follow the believer. Signs and wonders should be in your life at various times. As a believer, you have the Holy Spirit power and authority to use Jesus' name, perform the same signs, wonders, and miracles that Jesus did.

Jesus received the Holy Spirit and power to begin His ministry. Here is great passage of scripture I would like you to look at:

> *". . . how God anointed Jesus of Nazareth with the Holy Spirit and power, and how he went around doing good and healing all who were under the power of the devil, because God was with him."* (Acts 10:38 NIV)

Jesus did miracles, signs, and wonders and He gave the same authority to His disciples.

> *"When Jesus had called the Twelve together, he gave them power and authority to drive out all demons and to cure diseases, and he sent them out to proclaim the kingdom of God and to heal the sick."* (Luke 9:1–2 NIV)

Signs and wonders were not just for the twelve disciples; they are for us too. Here is an example of a person that wasn't a disciple, yet he desired to serve Jesus.

Stephen was one of the people selected to serve the disciples, wait on tables, and at the same time he shared Jesus' message and power. Stephen was a person just like us. As you read the below Bible verse, put yourself in this story as a servant, disciple, and follower like Stephen. Relish in knowing you can also perform great wonders and signs in Jesus' name.

> *"Now Stephen, a man full of God's grace and power, performed great wonders and signs among the people."* (Acts 6:8 NIV)

If you want to operate in signs and wonders, keep seeking Holy Spirit for guidance. He will use you as it is within God's will. You don't need to be a minister or pastor to do the works; you just need to be available.

REFLECTION

Look at the Bible carefully as you go through your week. Think about all the things that Jesus did. What would it look like in your community if His actions occurred today in your neighborhood? What would happen? What lives would be changed? Think about how powerful that would be and how it can happen through you.

PRAYER

> *Lord, please use me to do the greater works*
> *that you talk about in your word. Help me*
> *to rise with new expectation today to be your*
> *hands and feet in the world, and in my com-*
> *munity. Help the people around me that need*
> *you, and give them grace, and mercy. Allow*
> *me to give them your love to change their*
> *world. In Jesus' name. Amen.*

Battle Ready

"Then I said to you, 'Do not be terrified; do not be afraid of them. The LORD your God, who is going before you, will fight for you, as he did for you in Egypt, before your very eyes, and in the wilderness. There you saw how the LORD your God carried you, as a father carries his son, all the way you went until you reached this place.'" (Deuteronomy 1:29–31 NIV)

TODAY'S INSPIRATION

The Battle is not ours to fight alone. That is good news. Have you ever gotten into a fight of any kind and wished you had help? It could have been as a kid in a neighborhood skirmish, a financial battle, or health dilemma. It doesn't matter what the battle is, God is with you.

What an amazing image in the verse above of how much God loves us. He will carry us in times of trouble. If you are like me, you think all the battles are won or lost based on our own strength. God desires you to trust in Him daily for His power, guidance, and wisdom.

The battles we have are already finished and solved in Christ's death and resurrection. The fight has already been won with Jesus' blood on the cross.

When we try to take on the world and its darkness alone, we are ignoring what Jesus has completed for us and making His sacrifice of no value. God wants you to be aware of His cleansing power of the blood of Jesus and our salvation in him.

Your life in Christ is not one that you live alone. God has equipped you and me to be battle ready. Your battles are His battles. Your life and His life are deeply connected and intertwined.

How do we let Him fight our battles? Some things we go through we need to address them, handle them here on the Earth with his love and guidance. We need to talk to people sometimes that don't understand us or want to hear us. These things can cause battles within us.

What do we do? How do I fight if it is His battle? The way we fight is with His weapons. God gives us weapons that He says are not carnal; moreover, they are mighty and in pulling down of strongholds

(2 Corinthians 10:4 KJV paraphrased from). In this life, you are going to have battles, circumstances, and difficulties. You must handle these natural things with supernatural weapons.

Prayer is a battle weapon. You fight by drawing closer to God in prayer on your knees. Prayer is a supernatural weapon and will keep you battle ready.

Love is another mighty weapon. Loving those that are warring against you is a way to fight. God will begin to use that love to break down the enemy and his attacks against you. Your battles are not against people, they are against the enemy, the devil, and his demons.

Your battle is not with the things of this world, so your weapons are not of this world. Remember that when you struggle with a situation or person. Use the battle-ready weapons as shown below.

> *"Finally, be strong in the Lord and in his mighty power. Put on the full armor of God so that you can take your stand against the devil's schemes. For our struggle is not against flesh and blood, but against the rulers, against the authorities, against the powers of this dark world and against the spiritual forces of evil in the heavenly realms. Therefore, put on the full armor of God, so that when the day of evil*

*comes, you may be able to stand your ground,
and after you have done everything, to stand.
Stand firm then, with the belt of truth buck-
led around your waist, with the breastplate of
righteousness in place, and with your feet fit-
ted with the readiness that comes from the gospel of peace. In addition to all this, take up the
shield of faith, with which you can extinguish
all the flaming arrows of the evil one. Take the
helmet of salvation and the sword of the Spirit,
which is the word of God. And pray in the
Spirit on all occasions with all kinds of prayers
and requests. With this in mind, be alert
and always keep on praying for all the Lord's
people."* (Ephesians 6:10–18 NIV)

REFLECTION

Think about the battles you are in now or have been
in. What tools did you use? Did you use God's words?
Did you wear faith as a shield while fighting the battle?
God is here for you, ready to fight for you. He knows all
the parts of the battle and how to help you. Trust Him
today with your battle and be victorious.

PRAYER

Lord, I thank you for always fighting the battles as I go to you in prayer. I thank you for the spiritual weapons that you have given me and how I have victory in all things with you. I ask you to strengthen me and cause me to hear your voice in all things. In Jesus' name. Amen.

Victory Over Darkness

"For he has rescued us from the dominion of darkness and brought us into the kingdom of the Son he loves," (Colossians 1:13 NIV)

TODAY'S INSPIRATION

When Adam and Eve lived in the Garden, they had everything they needed. They were in a perfect environment with the presence of God walking with them. They were free and transparent with each other and with God. There was no darkness or hiding there. God walked with them in the cool of the day and they had perfect fellowship.

Adam and Eve disobeyed God and plunged humankind into a state of sin that God never intended us to be in. They ate from a tree that God told them especially not to eat from. You can find the full story in Genesis 2–5.

> *"And the LORD God commanded the*
> *man, 'You are free to eat from any tree in*
> *the garden; but you must not eat from the*
> *tree of the knowledge of good and evil, for*
> *when you eat from it you will certainly die.'"*
> (Genesis 2:16–17 NIV)

When they disobeyed God, they caused all of humanity to be in darkness and death of all humankind. The devil that tricked Eve became in control of this world and humankind was without hope (until Jesus). Sin and sickness ruled the world; therefore, God had a plan from the beginning of time. God already had the solution, Jesus. From the foundation of the world, God would send Jesus to redeem man back into a right standing intimate relationship with Him. As a physical man, Jesus came to die for all and purchase us back from the devil.

Jesus came and redeemed us back, we now have victory over the devil, sin, and darkness. Sometimes there may be a problem because people don't always know they can walk in victory. Many people still live in darkness because they lack knowledge. We need to set them free by sharing the Gospel, the Good News of Jesus Christ, our redeemer, and Savior.

What is victory over darkness? In the Bible, darkness is talked about in different areas. Darkness can be a sign that God is absent in your life; there may be a spiritual blindness to God, you may experience suffering and hopelessness. The devil trying to attack you with junk. Thankfully, Jesus gives the believer victory over every one of these areas because Jesus "holds the keys of death and Hades". (Paraphrased from Revelation 1:18 NIV)

All darkness is defeated at the death of Jesus, His blood shed on the cross and His resurrection. Receive the light of Jesus and walk in His ways for all eternity.

Because of the victory over darkness by Jesus, we are brought nearer to God as it says in 2 Corinthians 4:6 NIV *"For God, who said, 'Let light shine out of darkness,' made his light shine in our hearts to give us the light of the knowledge of the glory of God in the face of Christ."*

It is Jesus who takes away any darkness in your life and mine.

> *"When Jesus spoke again to the people, he said,*
> *'I am the light of the world. Whoever follows*
> *me will never walk in darkness, but will have*
> *the light of life.'"* (John 8:12 NIV)

We walk in victory because of what Jesus did for us. Celebrate! Jesus has taken you out of the kingdom of darkness and brought you into God's kingdom. You are rescued. You are free. You have Victory through Jesus!

REFLECTION

Think about God's loving goodness and how He rescued you from the kingdom of darkness and put you into the Kingdom of light with Jesus. You are the light shining brightly in this dark world.

Write three things that God has done for you that rescued you out of the kingdom of darkness.

PRAYER

> *Lord, thank you so much for redeeming me and the entire world in your name. I thank you that I walk in your kingdom and live victorious. Thank you for saving me from destruction and help me tell others of this good news. In Jesus' name. Amen.*

Old Becomes New

> *"Therefore, if any man be in Christ, he*
> *is a new creature: old things are passed*
> *away; behold, all things are become new."*
> (2 Corinthians 5:17 KJV)

TODAY'S INSPIRATION

I have exciting, good news for you. When you are lonely, feel broken, or have a sin-stained life, you can shed that old nature and trade it in for Jesus Christ's love for you, free of sins, with no strings attached.

Your old identity dissipates when you give your life to Christ. He wants to help you live for Him in a new and loving way. The verse above says that old things are passed away. That means, the old things you have no use for disappear with your new life in Christ.

We all have old stuff in our lives. We have it in our closet, car, attic, or basement. It is all stuff we usually do not have any use for. We can throw it out, discard it or have a yard sale and sell it. Sometimes the old things in our lives can be too disgusting to look at let alone deal with. We look and may think, "What is the use of this messy stuff in my life?"

Think about the things you used to do before you came to Jesus. When you come to Him you can give Him all those old messy things you have (not the old kitchen sink of course, just our messy thoughts and problems). Jesus takes it and makes it new. He takes your old desires and begins to give you new healthy desires. He takes your old ways and gives you new ways of doing things. Those old ways and old habits are traded in for new habits and ways. Jesus wants to take your old life and exchange it for His life in you.

Sometimes we need a do-over in our life. You can have that in Christ. (He gave me one!) You can start over and become new through Jesus Christ.

The new you can manifest gradually or suddenly. Jesus promised you a new life in Him. He never leaves you the way He found you, but He leaves you improved. When you meet Jesus, you truly have a new life. I am a living example of old become new. God took out my stony dead dark soul and gave me a soft tender beautiful new soul when I became "born again".

REFLECTION

Write a list of the old stuff in your life that needs to be discarded.

Pray to Jesus, confess, repent of your sins, turn from your old sinful ways and ask Him to come into your life and give you a fresh new beginning. See yourself with the old all gone and done away with. Begin to see yourself with a new life in Him with new goals and dreams in your future. Let yourself dream again. (If you have not received Jesus as your personal Savior, see the "Prayer of Salvation" at the end of this book.)

PRAYER

Lord, help me to live a new life that you have given me. Thank you for taking my old life and giving me a new life in you. Give me new desires and new goals to look forward to. I thank You for helping me walk in this glorious new way. Help me to desire your heart for my life and live only for you. In Jesus' name, Amen.

Blessed to Be a Blessing

"Dear friend, I pray that you may enjoy good health and that all may go well with you, even as your soul is getting along well. It gave me great joy to have some brothers come and tell about your faithfulness to the truth and how you continue to walk in the truth. I have no greater joy than to hear that my children are walking in the truth." (3 John 1:2–4 NIV)

TODAY'S INSPIRATION

There are times in our lives we meet people who change our lives and cause us to see the Bible come alive in our own life. I had a life-changing experience when I met Andy. He was my new brother in Christ, who lived on the streets of Las Vegas. Andy had one pair of pants that were too big for him and he had to walk holding them up so they wouldn't fall off.

I thought to myself, what a problem that is to always hold up your pants with one hand and then you would only have one hand available to use for other things.

Then I had a light bulb moment. My pants stay in place because I'm wearing a belt, yet they won't fall off if I remove the belt, why don't I give Andy my belt?

After I took my belt off, I called Andy over and said, "Hey, why don't you try this belt and see if it fits you?"

He took the belt from my hand and very carefully put it through his pant loops. I was watching anxiously, waiting, and praying that it fit.

He slowly put it through the loops (while trying to hold up his pants) and then he cinched it up past the hole I use for my waist and pulled it smaller and smaller. I am saying to myself, please, please God, let there be a hole in the belt when he pulls it tight to hold up his huge pants.

Finally, he gets it to the right size and then looks for a hole for the buckle. Hallelujah! There was a hole, and he was able to buckle up those pants and walk hands free.

We parted ways, he to his newfound life in Christ and with pants that now are snug at his waist and me returning to the hotel.

On my way home from Vegas as I was in the airport with nothing to do but waiting to board the plane, I saw a belt store.

I thought, "I have enough money to buy another belt. Should I buy a belt, or should I go beltless and think about Andy and what he had to go through?"

God blesses me so I can bless others, I reminded myself. So, I bought a new belt because if somebody else needs a belt, I will gladly give them the new belt. It may seem like a simple thing, yet it changed my life to realize how loving and gracious God is to give me overflow so I can help others.

When I look back on this event and continue to pray for my new brother in Christ, Andy, I felt God leading me to the following verse to help me understand better.

> *"If anyone has material possessions and sees his brother in need but has no pity on him, how can the love of God be in him? Dear children, let us not love with words or tongue but with actions and in truth."* (1 John 3:17–18 NIV)

Remember that God will use you no matter the situation. We are blessed, to be a blessing to others, and this can occur on the streets of your town, a store, work or anywhere.

REFLECTION

Is there anyone in your life that you can bless? Look around and hear Holy Spirit talk to you about a neighbor, friend, or co-worker today. Trust Jesus for the provision to be a blessing to them. You never know where it may lead them.

PRAYER

> *Lord, thank you for blessing me with provisions. Help me see who needs to be blessed today and use me to bless them and minister to them. Let me be used of you to be your hands and feet to someone in need. In Jesus, name. Amen.*

Price Paid

"*For the wages of sin is death, but the gift of God is eternal life in Christ Jesus our Lord.*"
(Romans 6:23 NIV)

TODAY'S INSPIRATION

When God looks at us, He has tremendous love for us no matter what we have done, He is a good Father. No matter the sin we commit or mistakes we make, God is love and that love is available to us all at any given time.

We have all sinned and will never be "good enough" on our own merits—God knows that. He has factored in the act of forgiveness for all our sins. Forgiveness for our sins always comes with a price. It is not free. Jesus paid the highest price of all for our sins. His death on the cross was the price He paid for you and for me.

In our life we will be called to pay a price and forgive others for random things. Let me give you an example.

I own a business and at times employees have damaged equipment, wasted materials, and broke things.

Recently one of my employees thought he was doing the right thing. It was a very cold day outside and he lowered the overhead garage door partway to try and keep some of the heat in the building and the cold air outside. He later jumped on the forklift and drove it towards the garage door and forgot it was half-way closed. As he attempted to go under the garage door with the forklift, the mast hit the lowered garage door that was above his line of vision, yet not high enough to allow for the tall mast to pass through freely. This action caused major damage to the garage door! Thankfully, the employee wasn't injured.

I forgave this employee for the mistake. Yet, I had to pay the price of the repair even though I did not cause the damage because I desired to restore the garage door to full capacity regardless of how the problem occurred.

Likewise, Jesus didn't do anything to cause our sin, however He paid the price for our sins. The sacrifice of His life was the costly price to redeem us out of eternal sin and damnation. Jesus loves us enough to fix, forever, our sin problem.

Because of Jesus, the price is paid for all eternity and that is good news.

REFLECTION

Have you ever had someone in your everyday life that paid a price on your behalf, and you didn't deserve it?

God said these words to us, "I forgive you." He paid a price for you. Think of three things that God has done for you as a pardon. Reflect on how much that cost Him for you to be free from that bondage.

You couldn't pay that price; you couldn't be good enough or do the right thing enough. Think about the freedom you have because of the price someone else, Jesus, paid.

PRAYER

Lord, thank you so much for forgiving me of all my sin. Thank you for paying the price for me and for all of mankind. I love you Lord and ask you to help me pay the price where I can for others and keep forgiveness in my heart for them. In Jesus' name. Amen.

Praying in Faith

"This is the confidence we have in approaching God: that if we ask anything according to his will, he hears us. And if we know that he hears us—whatever we ask—we know that we have what we asked of him." (1 John 5:14–15 NIV)

TODAY'S INSPIRATION

How do we have faith in our prayers? What does it mean to pray in faith? Sometimes when we pray it's hard to see the answer in the flesh. Our mind wanders and doubt can come in.

When we know God's will and use our authority that He has given us in our prayer time, we will see victory and our faith will grow stronger. Knowing God's will means knowing His Word. The more you know and take into your soul and spirit, the more your faith will grow.

Because of the finished work of the cross we are to use our authority and partner with God in the prayer of faith. Here is one of the prayers of faith that Jesus said:

> *"I will give you the keys of the kingdom of*
> *heaven; whatever you bind on earth will*
> *be bound in heaven, and whatever you*
> *loose on earth will be loosed in heaven."*
> (Matthew 16:19 NIV)

What does it mean to bind and lose? When you pray to bind you are tying up the evil. You muzzle it and make it of no effect. It is like tying someone to a chair, they are not free. When you lose something, you are setting it free and causing it to not be attached to evil. You declare the thing free and aligned with the will of God.

When you pray in faith you are praying the will of God and believing it with all your heart, mind, soul, and strength. When you do that, you release heaven's blessings that have already been promised through Jesus.

Keep your eye on the Word of God, have faith and imagine in your mind's eye the desired answers for which you are praying. Imagine that glorious result in your life and the lives of the people you are praying for.

The effective prayer that the Bible talks about is a prayer of faith as well. It is a faith-filled prayer meaning you receive the answer by faith before seeing it manifested in the natural. When this happens, you can stand firm, believe, and wait with perseverance without wavering.

An effective prayer is a prayer that stands up against the enemy. *"The effectual fervent prayer of a righteous man availeth much."* (James 5:16b KJV)

Here is a great verse to help you remember you must believe you have it, and it will come to you.

> *"Therefore, I tell you, whatever you ask for in prayer, believe that you have received it, and it will be yours."* (Mark 11:24 NIV)

Know there is no special recipe to make God obey and answer your prayers. There are only consistent faith-filled prayers. He is our mighty God and knows what you need and loves you dearly. Reach out to Him with your arms raised high in prayer and receive what He shows you.

REFLECTION

Think about a time that you know you asked God for something; your faith was high, and you received it before you physically had it. Think about the faith that you walked in that time. Reflect on how easy it was to believe and receive. God wants you to live like that every day. He is such a wonderful, loving God and wants to bless you before you see it.

PRAYER

> *Lord, thank you so much for blessing me and increasing my faith. I ask you to help me pray faith filled prayers of believing before I see it. Help my unbelief to be far from me and for me to walk in expectation of you answering my prayers and not doubting. In Jesus' name, Amen.*

Prayers Answered

"Ask and it will be given to you; seek and you will find; knock and the door will be opened to you. For everyone who asks receives; he who seeks finds; and to him who knocks, the door will be opened. "Which of you, if his son asks for bread, will give him a stone? Or if he asks for a fish, will give him a snake? If you, then, though you are evil, know how to give good gifts to your children, how much more will your Father in heaven give good gifts to those who ask him!" (Matthew 7:7–11 NIV)

TODAY'S INSPIRATION

God is in all things, even when they appear to be small, He wants to bless you and answer your prayers. When we pray, we must believe that He hears us, all the time.

Let me give you an example of how God answers our prayers even in the small things.

A few months ago, I was driving myself crazy trying to find my lost truck key. The last time I remembered having it was at a ministry event on a Sunday when it was in my pants pocket. That evening the wind swirled around the tall buildings of downtown Minneapolis and was so cold I had to wear my hoodie, three coats and a couple shirts to keep warm while I greeted people at the event.

Frantically the next day, I searched my laundry basket and pants pocket looking for the key. I searched the three coats I had on. Nothing. I searched my purse, the wall hook and trunk of my car with nothing to be found. I even asked my husband if he had the key.

I looked for three days and no sign of the missing key. I did, however, have an extra key I was using while I searched for the main key.

On the third day of looking, I finally stood in the laundry room frustrated and asked God where the key was. I knew He knew.

I prayed fervently. "Dear God! You know all things. You know where my key is. I pray today you show me where the Dodge Ram 2500 truck key is." I wanted to be specific in case He hadn't been aware of what I was searching for. I laugh at this now.

No sooner than I prayed, a thought popped into my head to go into the guest bedroom. Immediately my feet took off and I walked into the guest bedroom, opened the coat closet, my hand reached out and touched my black jacket. My mind questioned, *why are you touching that jacket, you weren't even wearing that Sunday when you had the key last*? I thought further, *I might as well check the pockets since I am here*. I felt within the pocket closest to me, emptiness. Then I reached into the closet to the far side, put my hand in the pocket and there was the key!

Tremendous love washed over me knowing even in the small things, God is there. Next, I am down on my knees crying out to God thanking Him for this miracle.

Yes, you can get simple answers to questions if you just ask Him. God cares about everything we go through. Even when we misplace our keys.

REFLECTION

Think about a time that God answered a seemingly small prayer for you. Try to remember a time when the answer came to you about something that you know you didn't know. God is a good Father and cares about what you care about. Trust Him today with the small things in your life.

PRAYER

> *Lord, thank you for helping me with the little things. Thank you for helping me with the stuff that doesn't really matter to others yet matter to me. I ask you to help me in all things of life and to help me remember you care about everything that concerns me. In Jesus' name. Amen.*

Holy Nourishment

". . . but whoever drinks the water I give them
will never thirst. Indeed, the water I give them
will become in them a spring of water welling
up to eternal life." (John 4:14 NIV)

TODAY'S INSPIRATION

Water nourishes our bodies and keeps us alive. We will not live more than a few days without water if we don't get it every day.

The living water of God is the same way. The Holy Spirit is the living water according to scriptures. It nourishes our soul. Jesus said that when we drink of what He has we will never thirst.

The human body thirsts for many things. Some of those things are bad and some are good. The spirit man thirsts for the things of God and without the Holy Spirit, we are walking around spiritually dead.

We need physical water to hydrate our bodies so we can physically function. We need the Holy Spirit to live our spiritual life now and for all eternity. What are you nourishing your life with? Just as you need water, you need living water more.

Imagine a beautiful river flowing gently past you. You stand on the bank next to a tall weeping willow and red maple tree. At your feet, there are colorful flowers, including some lilies and daisies. The roots of the trees are enjoying the moisture the riverbank water provides. The root systems of the trees are soaking up the much-needed water for life and health of the tree.

Now, imagine yourself wading into the river water. You can wear a life jacket or just lie on your back and drift in the water as the current gently takes you down river. Feel the weightlessness of the water.

God wants to take your burdens from you, as if you floated in the river with little effort. He wants to give you the nourishment of the Spirit, the living water as you fellowship with Him. Rest, hope, guidance, love, joy, and peace all await you in the effortless living water of the Holy Spirit.

> *"On the last and greatest day of the festival,*
> *Jesus stood and said in a loud voice, 'If any-*
> *one is thirsty, let him come to me and drink.*

> *Whoever believes in me, as the Scripture has said, rivers of living water will flow from within them.'"* (John 7:37–38 NIV)

God is there with you to nourish you with His Spirit and bring you to a place of sweet peace every day. Jump in the river with Him and let Him nourish you with His life-giving water.

REFLECTION

Think about how much time you spend getting nourished by God and the presence of the Holy Spirit. Are you getting enough time with Him to live a full, healthy life? Reflect on what you may need to change to live a more nourishing life with God this week. Make those changes and see what a difference it will make.

PRAYER

> *Lord, I thank you for filling me with your nourishing Holy Spirit who guides me each day and fills me to overflowing. I thank you for the life-giving water you freely have given me. Help me to live for you in the river of your love and your presence. In Jesus' name. Amen.*

119

Undeniable Love

*"Your love, LORD, reaches to the heavens, your
faithfulness to the skies. How priceless is your
unfailing love, O God! People take refuge in
the shadow of your wings."* (Psalm 36:5,7 NIV)

TODAY'S INSPIRATION

My husband asked if we could have prime rib for dinner.
Being the good wife, I agreed and thought it was a great
idea. I called the local restaurant, ordered and was out
the door to get our meal.

While I was driving to the restaurant, I was listening to one of my Bible college classes titled "Goal of the
Cross". During this teaching, the professor was talking about how Jesus showed her she is loved by Him
with falling stars and random dimes. She went into
detail and the story really made me want what she had.

I wanted to see Jesus' love in a very undeniable, earthly, tangible way in my life.

After I picked up our dinner, snacking on part of it, I continued listening to the teaching. I arrived at our mailbox, and I had a "chat" with Jesus about how cool it would be if He would show me, He loved me with a dime or whatever He wanted to do. I just wanted something tangible in that moment.

After parking and bringing our delicious food into the house, I walked into our bathroom to change clothes. As I was standing there, I looked to the left where we have our laundry baskets. My husband's laundry baskets typically look like a tornado had recently been through them, with clothes all over, and change from his pockets scattered on the floor. Not this night. I could see the bottom of his empty laundry basket; none of his clothes were on the floor. He did his own laundry!

I was so stunned about the clean area, however, that excitement didn't even come close to the thrill I felt when there on the clean floor sat one dime. The dime sang to me: *I LOVE YOU!* I still get goosebumps thinking about how Jesus showed me He loved me that night right there in the bathroom.

After walking into the family room, I asked my husband to put aside his dinner and come see something. I told him the whole story and showed him the one dime on the floor.

He told me that he did do his laundry and picked up all the change on the floor. He also said he would have picked up that dime, too, if he had seen it. I knew it was Jesus being good to me and leaving it there as a sign of His love for me.

The best part is, this is not a one and done. He loves to do these things for all His children.

REFLECTION

Have an intimate relationship with Jesus and reach out to Him. Tell Him you want more of Him. Ask Him to show you tangibly. Keep your eyes open for how He will show His love to you.

Think about a time that you desired the love of Jesus to be real to you. Was there a time that Jesus really showed you He loved you? Something big or small? Reflect on how much he involved someone else or showed you a sign that He loves you.

PRAYER

> *Lord, thank you for your unfailing love to me.*
> *Help me to feel and know your love for me.*
> *Help me to give that same love away to others.*

Let my life be an example of your love for me and to give love to others. Let me show others how much you love them by funneling that love through me. Help me to love as you love. In Jesus' name. Amen.

Sowing and Reaping

"With me are riches and honor, enduring
wealth, and prosperity. My fruit is better than
fine gold; what I yield surpasses choice sil-
ver. I walk in the way of righteousness, along
the paths of justice, bestowing wealth on those
who love me and making their treasuries full."
(Proverbs 8:18–21 NIV)

TODAY'S INSPIRATION

Did you know you get nothing unless you sow and then
reap for it? Farmers get no crop unless they sow seeds.
You get no paycheck unless you sow time and work.
Sowing and reaping are two things that go together in
this life.

Successful sowing and reaping begin with good soil.
Have you ever tried to plant a garden on top of a pile of

rocks? How about in clay? Perhaps sand? Nothing substantial will grow. Farmers know that the quality of the soil makes a huge impact on the amount they will harvest from the seeds they have sown into the dirt. Jesus was familiar with the importance of good soil for the seed and His Word to take root.

> *"Then Jesus said to them, 'Don't you understand this parable? How then will you understand any parable? The farmer sows the word. Some people are like seed along the path, where the word is sown. As soon as they hear it, Satan comes and takes away the word that was sown in them. Others, like seed sown on rocky places, hear the word and at once receive it with joy. But since they have no root, they last only a short time. When trouble or persecution comes because of the word, they quickly fall away. Still others, like seed sown among thorns, hear the word; but the worries of this life, the deceitfulness of wealth and the desires for other things come in and choke the word, making it unfruitful. Others, like seed sown on good soil, hear the word, accept it, and produce a crop — thirty, sixty or even a hundred times what was sown.'"* (Mark 4:13–20 NIV)

You determine what you sow, and you also determine what you reap.

Here is a simple example.

If you have an apple, eat it and do nothing else. But you will not gain prosperity from it. If you eat the apple and then plant its seeds, you will harvest apple trees. You now will have more apples with more seeds than you started with. Your reaping will be in abundance. The new apples can produce more seeds and more seeds means more trees.

Without good soil, a good foundation, and good dirt, the seeds cannot take root and grow. You will be stagnant, stuck in poverty, or depleted of a healthy life. Cultivate and keep your soil nourished. True prosperity is taking what you have, thanking and praising God for the blessings, and being a good steward. By planting a portion of it, you will gain great wealth for all eternity. This applies to money, relationships—tangible and intangible things.

When you share the gospel with others, you are sowing seed. The Holy Spirit takes the seed and waters it in a person's heart because you share, or sowed, it within them. Once they hear God's word and He waters it, the good news grows inside of them. They live a new life in Christ and the process should repeat as they share the Good News.

I encourage you to share the Gospel with five people. Then those five people can share it with five others, and so one. Bless others with what Jesus has given you, and you will be blessed.

To get started, consider: what does your soil (soul) contain? Does it have good nutrients in it or is it starving? Is your soil (soul) fertile and are you rooted in Jesus? If so, give Him away to others. (Trust me, you will not run out of Jesus to give away).

Begin today by sowing into others richly and you will reap the benefits for all eternity.

REFLECTION

Today, I want you to make a list of at least five people you can share Jesus with. Think of it as spreading the seed of Christ to them. Think about sowing and reaping in a deeper relationship with your family, friends and co-workers.

PRAYER

Lord, help me live as a Sower. Help me sow and reap a God harvest for the kingdom. Help me to love those in my path and sow Jesus to them. I thank you for blessing me so I can bless others. In Jesus' name. Amen.

Destiny and Purpose

"As it is written: 'I have made you a father of many nations.' He is our father in the sight of God, in whom he believed—the God who gives life to the dead and calls into being things that were not." (Romans 4:17 NIV)

TODAY'S INSPIRATION

Absolutely nothing is impossible with God. Today's scripture is a powerful testament to the faithfulness of God and making the seemingly impossible possible.

Abraham demonstrated great faith, yet he was a human, just like you and me. He was not special by any means; except he had great faith. Abraham had unwavering faith, trust in God and what God said to him. Because of that faith, God used him and through

Abraham a tremendous promise was realized in his life that we all are partakers of today.

What was this promise? Abraham and his wife, Sarah, were childless, and they were old beyond childbearing years. God told them they would have a child and that He would make Abraham the father of many nations. Now, here is what is unique and baffling about this promise. Sarah was naturally too old to have children. God made a promise to them that Abraham would father many children against the natural impossibility of her body to have a baby.

Let's look at the verses about Abraham's belief.

> *"Yet he did not waver through unbelief regarding the promise of God, but was strengthened in his faith and gave glory to God, being fully persuaded that God had power to do what he had promised."* (Romans 4:20–21 NIV)

Wow! How powerful is that? He never stopped believing, he did not waver. Regardless of his circumstances, despite the naysayers who laughed at him and Sarah, through it all, Abraham believed God.

You and I have that same capacity for victorious faith. We can believe for the purpose of our lives to come to pass against what we see naturally happening.

God knew the purposes He had planned for Abraham and Sarah. He knew exactly what was going on in their bodies, yet earthly reality didn't stop God from speaking a truth to an earthly impossible situation. God has designed great plans and purpose for your life as well.

Abraham's destiny was in the words that God spoke to his situation, for no situation is impossible for God. Not one thing is too hard for our God to do. Have great confidence because your purpose is already sealed in the heart of God.

You have completed your path to God's promise. You can choose to believe God against all impossibilities or give up and remain in the ditch. If you stay with God, you will not fail. When God speaks, it will happen.

How, might you ask? Keep praying to God to show you the glorious plans for your life, then make the corrections along the way. Obey His instructions given to you by Holy Spirit wisdom and you will stay on the road to your destiny, just like Abraham. Choose to believe His promises for you and be victorious! Keep your unwavering faith.

REFLECTION

Take time and meditate on 3–5 goals you feel God has placed on your heart, regardless of whether they seem impossible. Give them to God and see what happens.

Let your heart go back to past promises that God has given to you and let Abraham and Sarah's story of faith breathe new life into your promise. Can you see yourself achieving these goals? Imagine the finish line and claim your victory.

PRAYER

Lord, thank you for being the God of the impossible. I know you have a destiny and purpose for my life, plus you have a plan. Help me stay out of the way so you can drive and show me what you have destined for me. In Jesus' name. Amen.

Prayer of Salvation

"That if you confess with your mouth, 'Jesus is Lord,' and believe in your heart that God raised him from the dead, you will be saved. For it is with your heart that you believe and are justified, and it is with your mouth that you confess and are saved. As the Scripture says, 'Anyone who trusts in him will never be put to shame.' For there is no difference between Jew and Gentile— the same Lord is Lord of all and richly blesses all who call on him, for, 'Everyone who calls on the name of the Lord will be saved.'" (Romans 10:9–13 NIV)

If you have not received Jesus as your savior and given your entire life to him, pray with me now.

Lord Jesus, I confess I have sinned against you

and people, forgive me, I am sorry from the depth of my being. I believe you are the Son of God, was crucified, died, buried, and was raised from the dead for my justification so that I could be right standing before you. I believe your blood has washed away my sins, never to be seen again, and I am cleansed. I ask you to show me who I am in you; my identity in you.

Help me to grow my roots deep into you and help me understand the depth of your love for me. I trust you with my life now and for all eternity. I put my faith in your shed blood, Jesus. Right now, rescue me, heal me, deliver me, and set me free. I thank you Jesus.

I invite the Holy Spirit right now to baptize me with His presence and His person. You said in your Word you would never deny anyone who asks for the gift of the Holy Spirit. I am asking now, Holy Spirit come upon me now, with the glorious evidence of speaking in tongues. I desire your power and strength to live a Christian life with meaning and purpose all for the glory of God. In Jesus' name. Amen.

Next Steps

"So then, just as you received Christ Jesus as Lord, continue to live in him, rooted and built up in him, strengthened in the faith as you were taught, and overflowing with thankfulness." (Colossians 2:6–7 NIV)

Your life will flourish as you become rooted in Jesus' love for you, shine brightly, and stand your ground against darkness. When you embrace God's Word, the Scriptures, within this devotional and the bible, renew your mind with how much Jesus loves you. Begin to walk out His Holy Spirit power within you, in your natural daily life, which leads to victory now and for all eternal glory.

Trust God to do what you cannot do alone, because with Him all things are possible. *"Jesus looked at them and said, 'With man this is impossible, but not with God; all things are possible with God.'"* (Mark 10:27 NIV)

Stand firm, have faith, do not doubt, and trust ALL of God's promises. *"For no matter how many promises God has made, they are "Yes" in Christ. And so through him the "Amen" is spoken by us to the glory of God. Now it is God who makes both us and you stand firm in Christ. He anointed us, set his seal of ownership on us, and put his Spirit in our hearts as a deposit, guaranteeing what is to come."* (2 Corinthians 1:20–22 NIV)

Join a good bible-based church, worship, fellowship and continue to learn with other likeminded Christians.

Go in peace and claim your victory through Jesus now and for all eternity. Praise be to God!

Acknowledgements

First, thank you God for sending your Son, Jesus Christ, to save me (glory now and forever) and for giving me Holy Spirit to guide me as I wrote this devotional.

Next, my husband, who is always at my side, giving insight and suggestions that are priceless. We are opposites; therefore, his viewpoint is critical because I cannot see much that he sees. When he tells me his ideas, it is usually hard for me to understand at first because we are so different. I must digest it, along with Holy Spirit guidance, before it can bring fruit to the situation.

Cover art is by my beautiful creative daughter, Lacey Ballard. This design was a vision of mine from 2021 and I commissioned Lacey to draw what I could feel, my soul growing down into my spirit. As I continually pursued Jesus and knowing Him intimately this design became my soul's roots growing deep into Jesus.

Acknowledgements

It always feels good to come to the finish line. I want to thank my pit crew: editors Stephanie Carter and Judith Brenner as well as book designer Paul Nylander.

I thank God for the many wonderful people He put in my life, whether they are listed above or not, to cheer me on and share their talents with me so I could come to the checkered flag and complete what I set out to accomplish.

About the Author

Leslie Jackson is a traveling minister with a heart for winning souls, through Jesus, for the glory of God. She is a wife, mother, grandmother, retired race car driver, business owner, and enjoys driving her motorcycle and Corvette on the winding roads surrounding her country home in Western Wisconsin.

For more information, visit https://LeslieJackson.org